WORDS DANCE ^{14}
poetry mag

Fall 2013

WORDS DANCE PUBLISHING
WordsDance.com

WORDS DANCE 14
poetry mag

EDITOR-IN-CHIEF
Amanda Oaks

CONTRIBUTING EDITORS
Rebecca Schumejda
John Dorsey
Jessica Dawson
Jason Neese

© Words Dance 2013

All rights remain with the authors, always.

For more information, including submission guidelines, please visit:

WORDSDANCE.com

COVER ART BY
Jon Roueche

FEATURED ARTIST
photography by:

Seth Miller

POEMS BY:

- Donna-Marie Riley • Ethan Joella •
- Marina Oliver • Nathan Graziano •
- Carissa Callison • Adam Fieled •
- Nicola Cayless • Barton Smock •
- Jessica Dawson • Claire McMahon •
- Audrey Dimola • Dianne Borsenik •
- Jason Ryberg • Jennifer A. McGowan •
- Jennifer Stacy Kirkbride • RA Washington •
- Sarah Marcus • Steve Brightman •
- April Michelle Bratten • Claire Ibarra •
- Warren Buchholz • Jude Marr •
- Abigail Johanson • Susan Mahan •

An excerpt from Kris Ryan's book, *What To Do After She Says No*

PHOTOGRAPHY + ART BY:

- Johanna Falzone • Deb Taylor •
- Nara Denning •

cover art by JON ROUECHE

The art of Jon Roueche can easily be described as meticulous. His style, often featuring the butterfly, has developed through the years into a theme of rebirth and renewal. His current body of work incorporates bright watercolors and black ink.

After majoring in Illustration for four years at The Savannah College of Art & Design, Jon returned to his home state of South Carolina to pursue his artistic journey further as a freelance painter. His work is featured in the homes of collectors across the southeast, has been featured in several solo shows, and in Juxtapoz. His newest works are currently on display at Bob Doster's Backstreet Studio and Gallery in Lancaster, SC and can be viewed through his website at

JonRoueche.com

featured artist
SETH MILLER

Seth Miller was born in Wheeling, West Virginia, and currently lives in Ohio. He received a BA from West Liberty University in Graphic Design with an emphasis on Photography. In his more personal work, we see a style that's very emotional. He forces the viewer to see tension, anger, sadness, and struggle. Showing the emotions that society likes to look down upon in different environments is key to his style. Miller has worked in and around the music industry covering album art and tours. Using his visual style, Seth has traveled the country doing still photography and cinematography.

IAmSethMiller.com

ON CREATIVITY

When you find poetry in everything. When you twist words to carry vision to evoke a sense of feeling in your gut. When you plumb up goose bumps on skin.

When you watch the way the wind flirts with the grass, collides with your breath, sends a leaf tumbling down the road, turns the hair on your arms into marionettes spinning.

When you notice that sometimes you get in our own way. When you see that you are the silk cocoon wrapped around the hungry caterpillar of your own heart. When you know that the sinew sometimes binding you to fear doesn't weather rebellion well. When the hull of heaviness can either be added to or abated from the whole.

It's the process. It's the chase. Running down an inside revolution, footfalls on a sidewalk at night, chest heaving, heart at a full-tilt tick, the pull of the pin. The release.

The opening & closing of the shutter, five, ten, twenty times before you are at peace with the portrayal of the moment. It's capturing it on the first click. The last brush stroke sliding across the canvas. Ruled lines waiting for the warmth of your fist resting between words.

It's hitting your stride, stumbling, giving in, letting go, celebrating your victories & learning & loving yourself through your defeats.

It's the seed, the roots & the bud. It's the flowering of yourself.

It's the flow of our spirits dancing together through the seconds as they tumble off our self-imagined clocks. It's the meaning & the means to a meaningful life.

It only can be loved into action.

This is our courage unleashed, the moment the word YES sat on the edge of our lips, pondering, putting on her boots, standing up to spread her arms out wide only to

LET GO.

(Thank you for letting go.)
Love,
Amanda

Contentment | Mental Status Series | SETH MILLER

THE HEART OF THE MATTER

Let's tell the truth about the way we love each other. Let's display our bloody hands palms up, let the hunger in our bellies tell of our well-disguised violence. We never loved each other lightly. No, we never took the ballet classes our mothers signed us up for as children. We crushed beetles into dust, pulled grass up from its roots laughing. We showed too much teeth. We had voices of gravel, knees like skinned peaches. We signed letters under names that were not ours, forced people into forgetting us. You and I liked to set things on fire only to put them out. Still do. (Think of your loins, think of my temper.) Our fathers gave us BB guns instead of Barbie dolls. We shot down birds to examine their wings, buried them in old Metallica t-shirts and laundry detergent boxes. We love each other like that. We love each other limp; love each other 'til the water runs clear; love each other like a good, clean shot.

— *Donna-Marie Riley*

HIS WIFE TRIES TO ADD ME ON FACEBOOK

His wife tries to add me on Facebook. She wants to know if I am very beautiful, or worse, if I am less beautiful than her. The latter would hurt more. How can I be less beautiful than her and still have him write me letters about how he imagines my insides are made of silk? She wants to compare our faces, wants to find something wrong in mine. I will offer my big nose; offer my wild asymmetry; I will offer my skin that can't decide which country it belongs to. I almost let her in on the secret: I nearly reveal that I am nothing special. That's the real betrayal here. It is not that he has his desires. We all do. It's that she is so soft and pale and so close to a miracle and still, he is looking at me with his mouth open. Still, his blood rises when he sees me. I want to ask her if she is stubborn enough to place the fault on me. I have done nothing wrong, except for having dark hair and a darker character. I cannot help looking like a mystery. I cannot help looking like a loneliness that kissing alone would cure. I am not a weak girl. I'm no longer a weak girl and I'm no longer going to apologize. When the men bare their teeth, I do not raise my back like a cat. When the men drool, I don't squirm as if offended by my own attraction. When the men ask me to bed, I don't say yes. I don't break myself open for them. When the wives try to contact me, I don't bait them. I don't allude to my hips. I don't help them to imagine me naked. When the wives try to contact me, I write them poems. I imagine their bodies spilled over me like wine. I imagine loving them out of their marriage and into the safety of my silence. The men want me and I want their women, but the women are too intent on villainizing me in order to forgive the men.

— Donna-Marie Riley

DONNA-MARIE RILEY

Donna-Marie Riley is one part aspiring poet, ninety-nine parts self-doubt. She resides in Brighton, England and writes as a means of keeping the loneliness at bay. A selection of her work can be found on her personal blog: *five--a--day.tumblr.com*, whilst spoken word performances can be found on her YouTube channel. : *youtube.com/user/dreamlenore*

HANDS

My brother loved his music: Sex Pistols and the Smiths,
the park, graffiti-soaked skateboard, the cold ocean
unruly surfboard propped out the car window
Rip Curl, Mr. Zogs Sex Wax, white and black Vans,

his ill-fitting khaki pants, the girls who called
the house and said his name
with giggles in their voices, the park and his friends
at night, the short-lived jobs he kept: landscaping, ski lift

operating, party tent setting up , and I wrote
in my journal about him, knew he would never love me,
even though one of his girls said we had the same hands,
that our smiles cracked

the same way, and we shared turbulent eyes--
one night, in the room we shared, I coughed
into my pillow, the kind of cough that won't surrender
until you are awake again, propped up on pillow,

and there he stood over me, holding a white mug of water,
the ice cubes bumping against one another.
Here, he said, and I noticed his hands then, how much
they were my hands, holding for me the river.

— Ethan Joella

NEW JERSEY 1995

After the prom, we drove
two hours to Seaside Heights
in my red Volkswagen with
the bumper sagging.
Your curls brushed against
my arm as we lay towel
against towel in the sand,

sunburned and oil- steeped
in the May heat.
The boardwalk with its pizza
and *zeppoli* behind us. The clicks
of the spinning wheels where kids plopped
dollars on their number
and waited.

The boxwood green of
the water, the folding swells of waves
below. The man pulling a wagon
of newspapers, and two teenagers
propped on their elbows,
laughing about nothing—the hum of
the banner planes, the boats
in the distance, slowly moving
toward something.

— Ethan Joella

ETHAN JOELLA

Ethan Joella's fiction was a finalist for the 2010 Robert Olen Butler Short Fiction Award and the 2008 Eric Hoffer Award (that story appears in Best New Writing 2008). His work has appeared in The International Fiction Review, The American, The Delmarva Review, The Collagist, SNReview, Perigee, The Berkeley Fiction Review, Cicada (forthcoming), and Stickman Review. Ethan is fiction editor at Referential Magazine and a poetry reader at Ploughshares.

His website is : ethanjoellacommunications.com.

INSIGNIFICANCE

Softly across the ceiling you spin
silk stories in the shapes you wish for the world.

You say you feel yourself disappearing
against the knuckles of a skyline you once kissed

and I watch, eyes closed
as you fold inward, sticky skin barely gluing your seams.

I hang on your stories, your midnight musings
about feeling tiny and exhaling your dreams in short bursts.

We stare at the webs you wove between the cracks
in the ceiling's cement and interpret them like clouds—

You left a pair of collapsed lungs tangled in the left corner,
stuttering against the gravity of your own words:

I don't think anything I'm made of matters.
Your chest catches as you finally realize

the world never looks as bright as the final night
you felt you held weight against its rotation.

— Marina Oliver

FIVE TIMES I TOLD YOU

i.
I am sad.

She draws in her breath. It rattles in a way that reminds me of the week I had pneumonia.

"You have everything you need to be happy, but your cheeks hold white where pink should be splashed. If I had your freckles I'd never hide from the sun, I'd let them ripen until they were sweet and dark. You must not have tried hard enough to smile. You walk around trailing your clothes like a ghost. Buy something that isn't grey, buy something that sits snug around your hips so you have a shape. You simply are not looking at everything you have stretched in front of you. You were a beautiful child with blueberry eyes; you followed me around spouting curiosities into the air:

Momma, can I pick which flowers I want to plant in the garden this year? I told you yes, and you sat on your knees for hours digging in the dirt, kissing each seed before you tucked it away. Your flowers never bloomed that year, or any other.

Is that why you're sad? Because they never saw the sun?"

ii.
I am sad.

His reply came hours later (maybe days).

"Don't talk like that, like your knees are going to give out at any second. You won't be the one who will have to look at your body on the floor. Sit down if you're going to talk like that. Jesus, just—"

iii.
I am sad.

He doesn't turn his head from the television, but he presses mute.

"I know, you're the color of the Atlantic Ocean. But, you know, not in July when the families are crowding the beach and the kids are searching for treasures in the surf. Maybe in May, when you bring a blanket and let the salty air take the place of swimming.

You know, when you were younger and we took our van to the coast every summer, you never ran into the waves with your cousins. I'd find you, three hours later, spine curved over a tide pool. You would ask me to take a picture of you cradling a starfish, and I wasn't sure which of you was more silent.

I've never seen you run as fast as the summer we found hundreds of jellyfish drying on the beach. I told you it was just nature, but you pushed as many back into the sea as you could. I think I heard you crying on the way home, but I never asked. Your heart beat an extra measure for all the ones you couldn't save.

You had sunburn for weeks after that. Your shoulders turned into leather and yet I'm not sure if you ever managed to grow a shell."

iv.
I am sad.

We sit in silence. It sounds like choking when we try to talk.

She's sad too, I can see it in the way she walks in the mornings: elbows tucked into her sides, eyes closed. Next time, I will tell her I treasure the way her eyelashes touch the crowns of her cheeks.

When she calls at midnight, we always sigh before we say hello.

v.
I am sad.

Mirrors do not exist to solve riddles, only to show the dark circles beneath our eyes.

— Marina Oliver

MARINA OLIVER

Marina Oliver is a Creative Writing and Journalism double major at the University of Wisconsin—Madison. It took her awhile to weed out nearly every other major as a possibility and finally cozy up to the inevitable writing life course, but she made it. Her favorite things include music festivals, hearing about others' life journeys, frozen pizza, and vigilante social justice.
wordswecaptured.tumblr.com

ANOTHER FRIDAY NIGHT

At one time, on Friday nights, my thirst for your flesh
surged with every drink, my drunk begun and ended with you.
We sang songs on our porch, my guitar in need of new strings.

With hangovers the next morning, we'd take our kids
to a small breakfast diner by the hospital and wait in line
for fresh omelets and crisp bacon and endless coffee.

Tonight—another Friday—I get drunk in a cheap motel, alone,
with the drone of a television tuned to the news.
I sip bourbon from a plastic cup and try not to cry.

With a hangover tomorrow morning, I'll meet you at noon
to pick up the kids and take them for pizza at a restaurant
where the waitresses know me and the beers pour forever.

— Nathan Graziano

A FEW MORE BLANKETS MIGHT DO

I placed the air mattress beside the window
and I wake every half hour, shivering,
trying to insulate myself with more blankets,
shivering, knowing this room I rented
with utilities included meant I couldn't mess
with the thermostat. I couldn't control my climate.

Shivering, I suppose this is a real deal separation,
being apart until one of us hits a scratch ticket
and can afford to pay a lawyer. I've placed my wedding ring
in front of a school picture of our daughter,
smiling beneath a hot lamp and a studio background.

When we first got married, you were pregnant,
and we rented a slum apartment where the pipes
kept freezing in February, and we piled blankets
on our bodies, shivering together, a chorus of teeth.

— Nathan Graziano

NATHAN GRAZIANO

Nathan Graziano lives in Manchester, New Hampshire with his wife and two children. He is the author of After the Honeymoon (sunnyoutside, 2009), Teaching Metaphors (sunnyoutside, 2007), Not So Profound (Green Bean Press, 2004), Frostbite (GBP, 2002) and seven chapbooks of poetry and fiction. His work has appeared in Rattle, Word Riot, The Hawaii Review, Sententia, Night Train, Freight Stories, The Coe Review, and others. His latest chapbook was a collection of flash pieces titled Hangover Breakfasts and published by Bottle of Smoke Press. For more information, visit nathangraziano.com.

42 | Maps Series | SETH MILLER

CHILDHOOD PEAKS SEEN FROM AN AIRPLANE

I.   Mt. Adams

My fathers favorite peak,
the one that fits his brown eyes perfectly.
She was a rare treat;
stealing what breath was left
in our aching lungs after a long hike.
It seems like cheating to see her this way,
so effortlessly, just a drive to PDX
and a short wait, no sweat.

II.   Mt. Hood

Halfway to Seattle and she's still hidden,
like her false peak is a hunchback
and she's been banished to the bell tower.
Most days rain and fog acted as cloaks,
but sometimes driving over the 205 bridge
her familiar face came in full view
and all thoughts of traffic and groceries vanished.

III.   Mt. St. Helens

It's easy to ignore the volcano
in the backyard when she's silent.
Lost her presence before I was born,
hidden behind lesser mountains.

Hidden like the abuse, until it wasn't.
Stories pluming into existence,
covering childhood summers with ashy grit,
something that can no longer be ignored.
The mountain never forgets what is boiling
inside, every day gaining height unnoticed
by the untrained eyes in her shadow.

IV.   Sometimes...

...the drive into Vancouver surprises--
there she is, a reminder of silence.
Sometimes she shows up in Montana,
ash polluting rocky mountain air.
A fine dust on black robes,
the grit whispering *happy graduation*.
I know this ash will always fall from my mouth,
and sometimes, like Mt. St. Helens,
I let others see it. Waiting for my pen
to pick up vibrations like the needle
on a seismograph, sifting white noise
from what makes the ground shake,
from what turns stomachs into acrobats.
My eyes reach through a grimy plane window
for those peaks like my words reach
for the needle jump, hands wide open.

— Carissa Callison

CARISSA CALLISON

Carissa Callison was born and raised on the wet side of Washington. She received a BA in biology from University of Montana Western. While in college Carissa rediscovered a passion for words and hasn't looked back. Her work has been published at Twisted Ink and in The Nano Poem Collection Anthology.

Arias | Mental Status Series | **SETH MILLER**

FOR JODIE

When the moon was half-full, you put on your black eyes, unclasped your bra and fed me the hash you had in a second floor flat above South Street; but for the harvest moon, with eyebrows painted in and a liberal ethos you became an Earth Goddess, diaphragm faked, doing lines in my loo to let yourself go for once, off into ether, on top of me or beneath. Never for me were you real— you remained the whore you played as a kid, over and over again, suggesting the impermanence of the self in relation to a butcher shop's universe funneled and funneling into an abyss— no fun. This is just for me— the final major motion picture I can make of you for myself, and those unclasped around your alphabet.

— Adam Fieled

ADAM FIELED

Adam Fieled is a poet based in Philadelphia. His books include "Apparition Poems," "When You Bit…," and "Cheltenham." His books and press cuttings are being archived by the Poetry Library at the Southbank Centre, London.

XYLEM AND PHLOEM

Every Monday,
my mother waters the ferns
with my father's soul.

We potted them when we moved into
this shabby old apartment. It smells—
tobacco, old people, death.

We house desperation. Despair
lurks beneath the laundry sink.

Every evening after work,
my father talks to skeletons.
He counts pennies,
lays them on the bathroom counter.

My mother steals them,
sews them into jacket linings,
trouser hems.

I fall asleep to rain on the windowpane.
The ferns wither away.
Leaves crackling,
the colour of Autumn.

The ferns cling on, breathing
poisonous fumes—

like my father let my mother
claw into his skin;
a parasite living full.

— Nicola Cayless

THIS IS HER DICTATORSHIP

Mother drives the car
like she drives the children:
wildly, with abandon.

The steering wheel is choking,
the engine learns what it is
to hurt until you are no longer

what the mechanics said
you were. Mother screams in Spanish
because the children's ears are sandpaper

and the wheels are wearing thin.
Tucked into brother's pocket, I am small,
screaming so silently,

knowing that Mother killed us all
because I spoke so quickly out of turn
and bit the hand

that drives me.

- *Nicola Cayless*

NICOLA CAYLESS

Nicola Cayless is from Sydney, Australia, and spends most of her time writing poetry and drinking too much coffee. Aside from playing with words and reading sonnets, she works at Thistle Magazine as a General Editor, as well as writing on travel and screening the writing submissions. Nicola has been published in several literary magazines. More of her work can be found at moderateclimates.com.

Self-Portrait as Frida Kahlo | JOHANNA FALZONE

Self-Portrait as Kurt Cobain | JOHANNA FALZONE

Self-Portrait as Sylvia Plath | JOHANNA FALZONE

JOHANNA FALZONE

Johanna Falzone was born and raised in New Port Richey, Florida. Growing up in the nineties the influence of punk rock music, feminism, Nickelodeon cartoons, and Barbie took over Johanna's world. These forces influenced her attraction to pretty imagery that ranges from the grotesque to the overtly feminine. Her self-portraits create contemporary icons that blur boundaries between celebrity and self. These theatrical productions use color and narrative to create charming antagonistic paintings.
johannafalzone.com

Maps Series | SETH MILLER

EPISTOLARY

i.
no tattoo
until you're old enough
to love your mom

ii.
no staring
for long periods
at a flower
unless the flower
is fake

iii.
no bringing
the man
behind the stalled hearse
of my shadow

water

— Barton Smock

SANCTUM

mother: half parable, half untrue. at the time, I thought all mothers were mine. nights, my clear head bested me with the anxieties of another's children. by morning, school seemed redundant. while pregnant with me mother says she sensed I was always bawling. my insane father still hears her coming. his thought is a long hallway. painted shut

    his body is a door. its outside knob warms my hand
    with the knowledge

that in its brother
my brother
is naked.

— Barton Smock

BARTON SMOCK

Barton Smock lives in Columbus, Ohio, with a wife and four children. He writes daily at kingsoftrain.wordpress.com and has numerous self-published titles available at lulu.com, but if you send him an email at bartonsmock@yahoo.com he'll send you PDFs of said titles for free.

AMBITION

New words sprout like leaves
from lips. These secrets,
these overflowing mailboxes.

We can never really deviate from language.
Once upon a time we spoke in heartbeats,
and before that, in *imperceptible shifts*;
your mother's womb was the great translator.

We all sit, waiting on green wings,
disguised as something human,
just wanting to be believed;
when instead we should rush blindly
with flashlights
to fill the mangled blanks of silence,
shape the world with kept promises,
bind violent hands with honesty.

This could be your religion.

We stand beneath the stars,
forecasting rain, and miss the sky.
Action is the glory of impatience,
stamps itself onto outward-turned faces.
You are more than the sum of your
cut-and-paste conversations;
you are more than your hourly wage.
You need no revision.

In your silence I read epics.
I see a thousand poems in your eyes.

Come closer —
shed the strangeness of your skin.

This could be your baptism.

Give me a candle. No, don't light it.
I'll put it in my pocket
for safe-keeping. You never know
when we'll need a little direction.

— Jessica Dawson

ANATOMY OF A MOUTH

Honesty has no home in
that godforsaken hollow. There are
no small cabins built for comfort
at the edge of those lips.

He strikes a match, throws it
on a stack of foraged sticks.
His shadow roots and rises behind him,
against the trunks of trees.
For a moment he beams — he's a
looming statue, a monument of dreams;
the next he's scraping round the
gaping black of his mouth
for extra kindling.

— Jessica Dawson

JESSICA DAWSON

Jessica Dawson is a modern-day Wendy. She abhors self-promotion but requires an audience at all times. She reads the dictionary for fun, speaks only in degrees of sarcasm and is more vulture than falcon, really. Her book, Fossil Fuels, is available from Words Dance Publishing.

Nature's Pierrette | Mental Status Series | **SETH MILLER**

FOR A BEER

For a beer
I'd give you up
and not realize
I was doing it.

For a beer
I'd drive drunk
to get more beer.

For a beer
I'd blame everything on you
in a made-up fight,
to get to the bar
for a beer.

For a beer
I'd strong arm you
against the doors
 you closed
trying to keep me
with you
away from all the beer.

I can't tell you why,
I don't need you;
I'm happy here,
with my beer.

For a beer
I'd restrain you/stop you
from stopping me

on my way to
who knows where
for a beer.

For a beer
I'd damn near
bury you alive
with my addiction
until my lies
drove you damn near mad
for a beer,
I'd promise you all of this.

For a beer
I'd give you up
and never once
look back.

— Claire McMahon

CLAIRE MCMAHON

Claire McMahon has been writing poetry for many years. While studying at Naropa University, she had the good fortune of studying with Allen Ginsberg, Anne Waldman, Joanne Kyger, Gary Snyder, and Bill Berkson. At Naropa, she and writer Steve Roth founded the journal Make Room for Dada, which published some notable poets like Amiri Baraka, Charles Bukowski and Bernadette Mayer. She earned a Ph.D. from Kent State University in 2004. Since 2006, with poet Lisa Janssen, she has co-edited the journal MoonLit, which will have its final issue published sometime soon. She teaches creative writing occasionally at Tri-C and also works as an Associate Dean at ITT-Technical Institute in Warrensville Hts., OH. Her book, Emergency Contact, is available from Van Zeno Press, Cleveland. Currently she runs at monthly poetry workshop at Visible Voice Bookstore in Tremont.

EXCEPTIONS

There
comes a time when your fingers
are numb to touch or lack of touch,
and the lit ends of your candle
are not giving off heat, but just
smoke..
Your beloved *ennui*,
your dizzying pace,
they resolve
to nothing
so
suddenly –
it's jarring enough to
pluck you straight out
of your world,
like God had some
involuntary knee-jerk
or head twitch
that made you
unreal
again,
but only halfway –
and you are stuck,
insect in the amber –
spindly legs and
unfinished sentences,
grazing the air but
never able to give in
to either fate..

Stay dead or
break open,
neither seems
like a solution when you're
watching the world explode
behind you
in a mirror reflection –
but you can't seem to
focus on anything except
that smudge on the glass.

– Audrey Dimola

AUDREY DIMOLA

The first thing Audrey Dimola ever wanted to be was a trapeze artist, but acrobatics of the written word have always been closest to her heart. She is a poet, editor, journalist, and curator working in the New York City area, where she was (proudly!) born and raised. Audrey is the author of "Decisions We Make While We Dream," an original collection of poetry and prose spanning 2000 to 2012, and is currently diving headfirst into editing her second book, "Traversals." A lifelong writer and performer, she is fascinated by the alchemy of ache into art, and aiming always to stay wild and stay grateful. Find her online at audreydimola.com

I am open | DEB TAYLOR

WORDS DANCE 14
poetry mag

I am free | **DEB TAYLOR**

WordsDance.com

I am loved | **DEB TAYLOR**

DEB TAYLOR

Deb is a passionate photographer and blogger at What's Deb Doing. She resides near the beach in Merritt Island, Florida. Known as a peace-seeker, full-moon dancer, red-wine lover and daytime-dreamer. She also expresses her creativity inside the pages of her art journal, including mixed media and fabric arts. She hosts and teaches local workshops, as well as her own Mish Mash e-course. : *diddebdoit.blogspot.com*

KARMA CAFÉ

star*dust*
sifting through
the Karma Café

the earthly remains
of all we compose
or decompose

adrift
without a paddle
without a canoe
without a can-do
or can-you
or yahoo
without a beacon
from beyond
or before

just
being
just
becoming

stress
or should I say
the *dis*tress
of life
the sos
and yolo
of life
the lol
and wtf
of *life*

*does not get better
by chance*

(that's what I read
on a church sign
by the side of the road)

but by change
by driving
the convertible
of life
with the top
down

with the winds
of change
the rain of circumstance
and yes
the sunshine glance
of chance

blowing wild
through your hair

with the winds
of change
blowing through your soul

star*burn*
slipstreaming through
the Karma Café

under a full moon
mutual gravitation

me to you
you to me

responsibility and relationship
relevance and revelation
a cosmic dance
aswirl with possibilities

but you gotta be careful
you gotta know for sure

you have the universe's
undivided attention
and seemingly divine
intervention

so you gotta be convinced

be careful what you ask for

if you blow smoke
in the face
of the universe

it's going to smack your ass

— Dianne Borsenik

— I discovered the word "starburn" in the poem "Turning" by Jack McGuane, and credit him with first use of this delicious word.

DIANNE BORSENIK

Dianne Borsenik is active in the northeast Ohio poetry scene, and is founder/editor of NightBallet Press. She also cofounded the legendary Lix & Kix Poetry Extravaganza and Snoetry: A Winter Wordfest. Her poems have appeared in Slipstream, Rosebud, Nerve Cowboy, MiPOesias, The Magnetic Poetry Book of Poetry, and Haiku World: An International Poetry Almanac, among others. Her most recent chapbooks are Fortune Cookie (Kattywompus Press), Luminaria (Spare Change Press), and Blue Graffiti (Crisis Chronicles Press). www.nightballetpress.blogspot.com

THE SECRET HISTORY OF THE NIGHTTIME WORLD

Crows floating on a dark river of wind
winding deeper and deeper
into night's mysterious inland sea.

A bed-side radio channeling old transmissions
of The Shadow, The Lone Ranger
and Little Orphan Annie,
pulling street sweepers, star-quarter backs
and bank presidents alike
back into the shallow end of sleep.

A man stepping out of the side door of his life
and into a waiting pick-up truck
then down to the corner convenience store
for a liter of vodka and a carton of cigarettes,
never to return.

A mysterious strain of fortune cookies
giving the, fragmented, but true play-by-play account
of what really went down at Golgotha, Wounded Knee,
Nan King, Roanoke, Roswell.

The Man In The Moon
riding his shining black stallion across the sky
to his secret fortress at the bottom of Lake Tiachi
(known to the specially a-tuned as "Lake Of Heaven"),
where he will continue working all morning,
putting the finishing touches on his own secret history
of the nighttime world.

— Jason Ryberg

JASON RYBERG

Jason Ryberg is the author of seven books of poetry, six screenplays, a few short stories, several angry letters to various magazine and newspaper editors, and a box full of folders, notebooks and scraps of paper that could one day be (loosely) construed as a novel. He is currently an artist-in-residence at The Prospero Institute of Disquieted Poetics and an aspiring b-movie actor. His latest collection of poems is Down, Down and Away (co-authored with Josh Rizer and released by Spartan Press). He lives in Kansas City, Missouri with a rooster named Little Red and a billygoat named Giuseppe. Feel free to look up his skirt at jasonryberg.blogspot.com

ERAS OF LOVE

IGNEOUS
Our gazes ignite.
Over coffee, drinks, dinner,
obsession grows.
In too-short nights
we flow like lava
and burn to each other's touch.

SPONTANEOUS
Despite work
and other commitments
stolen moments
see speed-dial thumbed.
Flowers, chocolates, weekends away
just to see
the other one smile.

FALLACIOUS
You doubt my word
and I
that you had to work.
We check each other's phones.
Nothing we see
satisfies one way or the other.

CANTANKEROUS
The house gets colder.
Arguments the only heat.
Accommodation turns
to mute intransigency.
We huddle resentfully
on different sofas
watch strangers in cafes
and look for that first explosion.

— Jennifer A. McGowan

JENNIFER A. MCGOWAN

Jennifer A. McGowan was born in the US and raised predominantly in New England. She graduated from an Ivy League university with honours, and from the University of Wales for her M.A. and Ph.D. Despite being certified as disabled at age 16 with Ehlers-Danlos Syndrome, she went on to become a semi-professional mime and performed in five countries. She has published poetry and prose in various magazines and anthologies, and has both written and recorded songs on several (small, but perfectly formed) labels. She loves teaching and has taught both under- and postgraduates at several universities. Having been resident in the UK since 1992, she recently naturalised.
jenniferamcgowan.com

MAGPIES IN THE MORNING

swooping above my head
      all the way to the greenhouse
a tackle box full of seeds
      and my trowel

last night
      you held my hands in the sink
and scrubbed with pumice
the dirt embedded in my skin

and later
      we hosed the caked compost
and horse manure off our boots

The magpies know we are safe
      but warn anyway
as we coo back
and agree

I wear your clothes now
and we smell like family.

— Jennifer Stacy Kirkbride

JENNIFER STACY KIRKBRIDE

Jennifer Stacy Kirkbride can't snap her fingers, but can thread a sewing needle in a matter of seconds. She is a writer, personal trainer and the creative tea mixer behind Linen and Leaves. She is currently working on a collection of short stories. Born in Northern Ontario, the influence of the northern landscape is a prevalent feature in her writing.   linenandleaves.com

SIMONE (AT CIMETIERE DU MONTPARNASSE)

You guard their graves as kin.
tiny pebbles outside the gate
like flecks of glass.
shards beyond us, in the folds
of what's been read.

so many stones
unturned to find us here.
the year Simone died, 1986
You were not yet 22.
just fresh out of terror
as I was just to enter.

(there is no crime worse than fathers.)

and I've come to hold You.
here at their grave.
a note for Simone
weighted under pebble
for nights she told You–
"this is my model
for saving one's self."

– RA Washington

RA WASHINGTON

RA Washington lives with his wife, Lyz Bly on Cleveland west side, and runs Guide To Kulchur: Text, Art & News, a used bookstore/zine co-op located in the historic Gordon Square Arts District. He has published over 20 books, and is dedicated to independent publishers, and small presses. facebook.com/GuideToKulchurCleveland

NO ONE SAW THE MOON THAT BLED IN MY MOUTH

There are places where land falls into sea.
He says you are so warm and wet and tight
tenderly, as if the winds could rest at any moment.

Their kiss crosses Mokallah beach
each time water meets land. An echo
of suffering, a rain shadow of hurt
dampening the other side.

There's a place she'd like to show him, relief
in that landscape, somewhere lush and untouched.

The desert's singing sands haunt her at night,
so she pushes against him, and though he's sleeping,
he brings her in hard.

She's wild—stays there unbroken
until the birds settle into the tree line.

When the winds break, his color will return,
and the bite of morning will be on her.
She will ask for the memory of him,
the fever of night.

— Sarah Marcus

NO CHILDREN

Family in the other room
quietly discussing
who will give
dad a kidney.

The old house shadowed
by trees. The bending
begins. Windows still spotted
from the night's cold rain.

All I can do is scrub the kitchen.
Eyes burning with citrus.

My sister says we should
move him to the sea
where it's peaceful,
where she lives.

My father will never leave.
The sea is just another desert.

*

My sister and I drive downtown.
Cleveland is one big hospital.
A series of parking lots and dark roads
decaying. Being here breaks my heart.
I imagine things in black and white
because it's sadder.

When people talk about Cleveland,
people who love it, people who

decamped to the suburbs,
they use words like rebirth and revival.

*

We try to have dinner with old friends.
We catch each other up
on almost weddings
and coming back homes.

What our parents did to us.
We say, look how incredible
we are despite them.

We laugh and nod. I touch my face
and remember the hurt of those days,
but don't dare say it.

I look at my sister, touch her shoulder,
and say, we will be better parents,
and, are you still dating that asshole?

*

I wish it was summer.
Mother's porch is paradise.
Flowers, tomatoes,
squash, peppers,
wicker tables, rocking chairs—

Outside, winter takes another tree
holding space
for a sacrifice
we haven't made yet.

— Sarah Marcus

SARAH MARCUS

Sarah Marcus is the author of BACKCOUNTRY (2013, Finishing Line Press). Her other work has appeared or is forthcoming in McSweeney's, Cimarron Review, CALYX Journal, Spork, Nashville Review, Slipstream, Tidal Basin Review, and Cold Mountain Review, among others. She is a guest blogger for So to Speak: A Feminist Journal of Language & Art and a Count Coordinator for VIDA: Women in Literary Arts. She holds an MFA in poetry from George Mason University and currently teaches and writes in Cleveland, OH. Read more at sarahannmarcus.com

Boots | NARA DENNING

The Nap | **NARA DENNING**

NARA DENNING

Born in San Francisco in 1976, Nara Denning is a native of the fringes and seeker of invisible realities. She has made a body of work which interprets what she has so far encountered, collecting antique elements to create seductive, turbulent dreamscapes inspired by personal memoir as recalled by the symbolic language of the heart. Denning creates a heightened reality that merges the external and internal experience. Her current film series "Under the Pavement" explores identity crisis in the modern age. Denning was awarded "Best New Silent Filmmaker 2009" by the SF Weekly as well as the 2010 "Investing in Artists" grant from the Center of Cultural Innovation and the 2011 Individual Artist Commission Award by the San Francisco Arts Commission. : naradenning.com

THEIR MORAL BONES

The words, they line up
like soldiers or saints,
waiting for their turn.
They enlisted with
their right hands raised
toward God and know
that they serve a higher purpose.
They can feel it
in their moral bones.
They live to die,
just like all of us,
but a little more eager.
The words, they tense up
once the marching orders
are sent from the comfort
of an underground bunker.
They wait to fill the page.
They have a legacy to fulfill.
They have a story to tell.

— Steve Brightman

THERE IN THE IN-BETWEEN

There are hours,
thousands of them,
that need to be spent
slowing the world down
to a processable speed.
It takes some time
to learn to see
the action in inaction.
It takes some time
to learn to see
there is more to it
than the wind-up
and the umpire's call.

There is sunlight
there in the in-between.

And sunlight is no
mere opposite of dark.
She is the brutish
cleaver of the mundane
and the unimaginative.
She is the brilliant
disguise of hiding
amongst the obvious.

— Steve Brightman

STEVE BRIGHTMAN

Steve Brightman lives in Kent, OH, and frequently worships at PNC Park, the finest cathedral in North America. His poems have been featured in Pudding House, Origami Condom, A Trunk of Delirium and he was included in the Ohio Bicentennial Anthology titled "I Have My Own Song For It: Modern Poems about Ohio."

SONG-LESS BIRDS

You were not supposed to die, boy.

You were not supposed to
haunt me in my sleep,
your eyes touching me
like Eastern bluebirds,
your hair, white.

You cannot speak to me now,
but I pretend that you do.
I pretend that the little chirp outside
the window is you.

I find ways to make
your eyes come to me
like a kingfisher over water.

I find ways to make you speak.

★★★

I send my body over the sea.
I wait for you over the sea.

But this is not England. This is not Germany.
This is not Israel.

This is America.
The birds here do not call.

I wait for you and bleed
when it hurts the most,
where it hurts the most.

I walk barefoot through rubble,
my skin dirty and aching.

I cry under light.
I cry under the yellow sky,
but it is not enough.

The sad song of a ghost-bird
is never enough.

– April Michelle Bratten

APRIL MICHELLE BRATTEN

April Michelle Bratten is currently living/trapped in the oil boom town of Minot, North Dakota. Her full-length poetry collection, It Broke Anyway, is now available from NeoPoiesis Press. Her second collection, Thin American Bread, is searching for a publishing birth mother. She co-edits the online literary journal, Up the Staircase Quarterly. : upthestaircase.org

A FORMULAIC LOVE STORY

[H_2O]

She is a lovely mermaid; he is Poseidon. They are still young.
Salt water heals wounds, so they bathe together during low tide for hours on end.

[$AgBr$]

They are sensitive to all things of consequence. Images become
clearer in their dreams, only to fade into phantoms, like the shroud of Turin.
They can't remember the details, of all they meant to say.

[Al_2CoO_4]

She dreams of living inside a Maxfield Parrish, with gold-rimmed clouds and
luminous skies of iridescent blue, the color of Chinese porcelain, of tinted glass.
It's the color that makes her happiest.

[AlO]

Exploding grenades. He was trained to deny love. You can't kill another human being
while believing in it. Now he lives with PTSD. She gives him renewed hope, nurses his
spirit with the droplets of a slow and gradual baptism, a baptism of an ancient love.

[N_2]

If it is not solid, if it doesn't fit into the palm of her hand, it will float out of the
atmosphere and disappear into empty space. That has always been her fear.

[CH_3COCH_3]

She keeps her nails long, and they click against cups and scratch his flesh,
giving him shivers. She wears blue polish. She uses yellow rubber
gloves to wash the dishes.

[FeO]

He can't write without a delete button. Permanence never suited him.
The Earth's crust is tattooed with etchings, the stories of loss and extinction.
Her stories will become etched in sunspots and wrinkles—his in a receding hairline.

[B(OH)$_3$]

The cruelty of sprinkling acid on fire ants nags at her—and yet she knows they can be
deadly. She marvels that something that can cure athlete's foot
also slows the rate of fission. She believes their love is a lot like that.

[CH$_3$CH$_2$OH]

Alcohol is the oldest recreation known to man, even Neolithic people drank spirits.
Residue was found on 9,000 year-old pottery in China. How can she argue with that?
Scientific evidence supports his cause.

[CH$_2$O]

They cling to each other after death visits. Though his drinking gets in the way.
But how can she deny him those sips of comfort, those sips of redemption,
those sips of forgetting pain.

[O$_3$]

They are protected from ultraviolet rays. The atmosphere is inviting,
as he watches her belly grow. They bask in the Florida sun and
their extended family becomes tolerable. They discuss moving to Kansas.

[I$_2$]

The sea is rich, and so they continue their bathing ritual at low tide, and
she buys iodized salt. Most anything can be purchased fortified.

$[As_2O_3]$

In the highest altitudes of the Alps, live the "arsenic eaters of Styria"
who believe the poison gives them strength. Arsenic is homeopathic.
There's a risk to cures, there's a risk in loving someone too much.

$[Fe_3O_4]$

When they first met, he had a moustache, a beard, and
abundant dark chest hair. She loved to twirl it around her fingers.
He was a man, she felt like a little girl.

$[H_2]$

He tells her that he wants to jump out of a plane on his 50th birthday.
Parachuting, parasailing, hot air balloons. Air travel will get him nowhere.
She knows what he wants is elusive.

$[Au(OH)_3]$

Their wedding bands are inscribed with the date of their anniversary,
lest they forget that day. Forget the years joining like molecules,
into formulas of strange and magnificent creations.

– Claire Ibarra

CLAIRE IBARRA

Claire Ibarra's poetry has appeared or is forthcoming in Thrush Poetry Journal, Blue Fifth Review, Poetic Pinup Revue, and Lummox. She is also a contributor to the poetry anthology "Point Mass" by Kind of a Hurricane Press. You can learn more at claireibarra.com

WEDNESDAY MORNINGS ON THE TERRACE

I get it--
that kind of
love
doesn't come
often enough,
and as I stare
from the terrace
to the tree tops
engulfed
in rain
and to a city
no longer
visible,
I remember that
look you've had
in your
eyes
all these weeks;
a glistening
lamentation
for someone else
lost like
those city lights.
I know
I can never
have you,
so I turn to
the plant next
to me
and water it.

— Warren Buchholz

WARREN BUCHHOLZ

Warren Buchholz has recently been published in magazines such as Zygote in My Coffee, The Legendary, Straight Forward Poetry, and Heyday Magazine. He is currently getting his B.F.A. in communicative performance studies at University of South Florida; performs improv and does marketing in a comedy group, Post Dinner Conversation; and also runs a comedy troupe, The Skitsaphrenics, for which he writes and acts. In his spare time, he masturbates.

ESCAPE

Scrape sky off of your shoe.
Pull weeds out of your hair. Wear
gray fatigues.
City streets bleed dust. You will
disappear—

Hear greed spill into cracks. Don't
look back. Don't
relax. Wind wire around your heart. Be
smart. Never
unplug used from user. Choose
a room without windows—

Wind blows. Garbage
huddles under
bridges.

A city keeps   (secrets)

– Jude Marr

DOWNHILL WITH KEROUAC

doorstep road, cobbled-over cloud, going nowhere but
to where peregrines freefall, ragged-winged, talons red-tipped—
to where radiant vapor-shifts make effigies, wisp-white, peace-pipe
puffs of evaporated coffee-steam—to where stray similes
stream like banners, wind-snapped to attention as day breaks,
cool blue at altitude—doorstep road least traveled, as heat eases in
between crags, as muscle-memories unravel into near-sleep
deliver me to radical astonishment. Skin-dreams, crisp intimations:
soon enough mere need will dislodge me from perfect pleasure
in refracted dazzle, and I will move to meet my self, scrolling
backward toward complicity, toward city streets. Already I can
feel a beat of kestrel wings trapped in tunnel traffic. Already
I can see blood pooled, immaculate, under me—under my purest
notes—and in my throat, I hear wheels rattle—

— Jude Marr

JUDE MARR

Jude Marr is a teaching fellow at Georgia College in Milledgeville, where she is in her third year of a poetry MFA. Her work has appeared in The Cortland Review and r.kv.ry., amongst others. When not writing or teaching, Jude reads for Arts & Letters and she is an assistant editor at the online journal Ghost Ocean.

Fervent Stacks | Mental Status Series | **SETH MILLER**

THE GIRL (ARIZONA) PTS. I & II

i.
She's wearing a mask
of red earth and sunbleached
leaves
PUREGODWHITE leaves –

a leucistic deer
leaving red tracks on new
snow.

Her mouth is
a dry birch leaf,
it turns over itself –
a dust-devil caught by her face.

ii.
'Me, I'm in love with Vermont,'
The Arizona Girl admits
(her body is pure duende her
throat is a rainwet tree)

'It's so beautiful.'
The Arizona Girl sighs,
hand curled under her chin she
has fashioned herself a dress of maple leaves
walks like a fawn
into spring, a shape –
shifting godcoyote
in the night.

'I am tired of being here.
I want to go home',
she flattens herself
with displeasure;
timbersnake
caught
in a northeastern winter.

– Abigail Johanson

ABIGAIL JOHANSON

Abigail is a 21 yr old poet and visual artist who lives near Kansas City, MO with her madhairedpoet husband Jacob, his four fantastic daughters, a dog, a cat, and four silly ducks. Their current obsession is sustainable living, and they're soon to be joined by chickens, quail, and a whole slew of rabbits. God bless 'em.

PICTURE THIS

It is May of my senior year of high school.
We are standing in front of the mirror in
the girls' locker room.

I am combing my hair. She is applying lipstick.

"*It's snowing down South,*" she says.

What I notice is that she is not looking at me.
Her eyes remain on her task, outlining, then
filling in the contours of her pouty lips with
Frosted Pink Powderpuff. She is not interested
in what she has just said.

What I think is:
*She's the most popular girl in school and
she has never spoken to me in four years.
Why is she giving me the weather report
in Alabama or Georgia?*

But, I defer to the image, which is irresistible:
It's snowing down South. I picture a cadre
of cotton pickers commencing a snowball fight,
building a snowman, making snow angels
without coats, hats or gloves because
it must have been unexpected.
Would a freak snowstorm kill the crops
and ruin everyone's livelihood?

I stare at her as she repeats,
"Did you hear me?"
Still no eye contact.
She blots her lips on a tissue.

*"It's snowing down South;
you know--your slip is showing."*

— Susan Mahan

SUSAN MAHAN

Susan Mahan has been writing poetry since her husband died in 1997. She is a frequent reader at poetry venues and has written four chap books. She joined the editorial staff of The South Boston Literary Gazette in 2002. She has been published in a number of journals and anthologies.

Self Portrait - Contradiction | Mental Status Series | **SETH MILLER**

I.

PUNCH

symmetrical holes in the

drywall of your room
. . . .
drywall of your skin

to match the broken line on a highway, something a pair of scissors can cut through swiftly.

VACUUM-PACK

of yourself

so flat you can fit
under a door.

Tack the other half
to power line poles
across town like
lost dog ads.

This is mashed-potato
masochism,

   beaten
      and spun
         and flung
           and stuck
              to the wall,

that merely multiplies
when cleaned.

Deal with it the way any
perfectly reasonable person
would—

>tape her picture
>on the bullseye,

then throw knives until you
puncture her eyes.

II.

CRY

into a pillow

until the case is soaked enough to smother and drown you at the same time, so that each one cancels the other out.

Realize the impossibility of suicide by either—

the body's panic response would never allow for it.

Thumb through the phone book for a name suitable enough to help carry out the act.

STOP

at every name

that rhymes with, is an anagram of, is a variation of, or just flat out *is* her name.

Rip out every instance
on every page

and

wallpaper your bedroom
with them.

Feel, finally,
that she is near.

is like watching your heart pound outside of your chest. Both an unsettling visual experience and a hurricane of sadness and rebirth—this book demands more than just your attention, it takes a little bit of your soul, and in the end, makes everything feel whole again.

- JOHN DORSEY
Author of *Tombstone Factory*,
Epic Rites Press, 2013

What to Do After She Says No is exquisite. Truly, perfectly exquisite. It pulls you in on a familiar and wild ride of a heart blown open and a mind twisting in an effort to figure it all out. It's raw and vibrant... and in the same breath comforting. I want to crawl inside this book and live in a world where heartache is expressed so magnificently.

- JO ANNA ROTHMAN
MA, Coach & Conjurer of
Electric Creative Wholeness

What to Do After She Says No takes us from Shanghai to the interior of a refrigerator, but mostly dwells inside the injured human heart, exploring the aftermath of emotional betrayal. This poem is a compact blast of brutality, with such instructions as "Climb onto the roof and jump off. If you break your leg, you are awake. If you land without injury, pinch and twist at your arm until you wake up." Ryan's use of the imperative often leads us to a reality where pain is the only outcome, but this piece is not without tenderness, and certainly not without play, with sounds and images ricocheting off each other throughout. Anticipate the poetry you wish you knew about during your last bad breakup; this poem offers a first "foothold to climb out" from that universal experience.

— *Lisa Mangini*

10.00 US
Poetry

WordsDance.com
Cover Design : Amanda Oaks

ISBN 9780615870045

Fossil Fuels

Poems by Jessica Dawson

CLOSE COVER BEFORE STRIKING

Introduced by her husband in a sweet and cynical tribute, Jessica's first collection of poetry captures the intimate lyrical confessions of a writer who seems unsure of the value of her confession, while at the same time certain that she must put them to paper, no matter.

"Overall, the collection delights and dances and mourns and shouts and sings and rejoices in what it is to be mortal and cerebral and receptive and observant in these difficult days...This is a ravishing and enchanting chapbook."
- Corey Mesler, *Author*

"...bold, direct, and unapologetic"
- Michael Gentilucci, *Editor, Slurve Magazine*

15.00 US
Poetry

WordsDance.com
Cover Design : Amanda Oaks

I DREAMT I WAS AN ALLIGATOR

all teeth and hot,
wet breath stomping about
on my new-found squatness.
My body was torpid, outward elbows
moving skyscrapers, that
scene in a nightmare
where the director Slows. Everything. Down.
for effect.

But then, everything
was vibrant, crashing

and I was *alive*
mud-yellow ivories snapping shut
on the rubber tent stake
of a flamingo leg,

feathers muffling the splintering noises,
crumpling pink and red on my tongue.

Jessica Dawson is a modern-day Wendy. She abhors self-promotion but requires an audience at all times. She reads the dictionary for fun, speaks only in degrees of sarcasm and is more vulture than falcon, really.

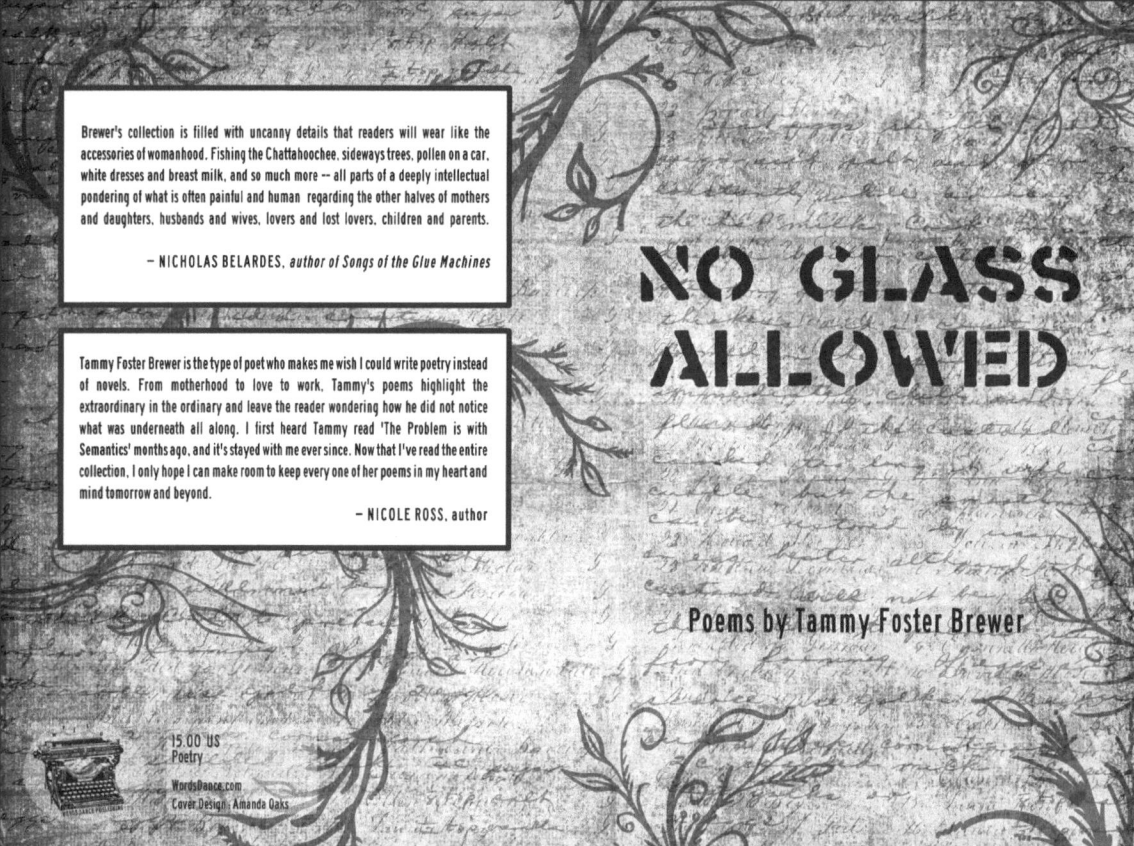

Tammy F. Brewer is married to the poet, Robert Lee Brewer, and is mom to 2 sons, 2 stepsons & a daughter. She received her BA in English from Georgia State University in 1997. She was born, raised, and still resides in Atlanta, GA where she works as a paralegal.

THE PROBLEM IS WITH SEMANTICS

When I say my appendix erupted
I mean my parents divorced when I was 8.

When I say I am a mom
I mean don't run so fast.

When I say I am stuck in traffic
I mean I need to call my sister.

When I say I am in love
I mean the moon, the stars, the sun.

When I say I am sorry
I mean let's take the stairs.

When I say I am a poet
I mean my house has many windows.

When I say I don't have the words
I mean shut up and kiss me.

www.ingramcontent.com/pod-product-compliance
Lightning Source LLC
Chambersburg PA
CBHW041703160426
43202CB00003B/17